501 Tips for Teachers

SECOND EDITION

ROBERT D. RAMSEY, ED.D.

Contemporary Books

Chicago   New York   San Francisco   Lisbon   London   Madrid   Mexico City
Milan   New Delhi   San Juan   Seoul   Singapore   Sydney   Toronto

Library of Congress Cataloging-in-Publication Data

Ramsey, Robert D.
        501 tips for teachers / Robert D. Ramsey.—2nd ed.
             p.   cm.
        ISBN 0-07-140988-2
        1. Teaching—Miscellanea.   I. Title: Five hundred one
     tips for teachers.   II. Title: Five hundred and one tips for
     teachers.   III. Title.

     LB1045 .R24   2003
     371.102—dc21

                                    2002074085

Cover and interior illustrations copyright © EyeWire, Inc.
Interior design by Susan H. Hartman

1 2 3 4 5 6 7 8 9 0   LBM/LBM   1 0 9 8 7 6 5 4 3 2

ISBN 0-07-140988-2

This book is printed on acid-free paper.

Contents

Introduction

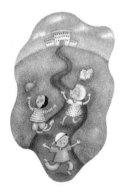

*"What office is there which involves
more responsibility, which requires
more qualifications, and which ought,
therefore, to be more honourable, than
that of teaching?"*

—Harriet Martineau

*"Teaching is not a lost art, but the
regard for it is a lost tradition."*

—Jacques Barzun

George Bernard Shaw said,
"Those who can, do; those
who can't, teach." George was wrong.

Today's teachers have to be doers.
They also have to be dreamers, schemers,
helpers, healers, mentors, role models,

nurturers, and inspirations. Teachers are expected to be dynamite every morning and to grade papers every night. Shaw was off the mark.

Teaching today isn't for wimps, wanna-bes, or also-rans. It's society's most important, challenging profession, and it's getting more difficult all the time.

In classrooms at all levels, problems are proliferating and expectations are escalating. Schools across the country are being called on to do more with less. Consequently, teachers everywhere are now looking for new sources of information and motivation.

Fortunately, help is available. Sometimes, the cavalry comes in the form of a little book filled with big ideas.

To succeed today, teachers need bold new ideas for helping and handling kids, as well as timeless insights into the nature of successful teaching and learning. *501 Tips for Teachers* offers both. It is a sanity-saving resource for teachers of all subjects and grade levels.

This powerful collection of school-tested teaching techniques, classroom management strategies, life-tested affirmations, and everyday encouragements has been gleaned from a career-long association with successful teachers at all levels. It includes fresh ideas whose time has come, coupled with reminders of surefire, established methods that never fail.

Used as an ever-ready source of coaching and encouragement, *501 Tips for Teachers* can help make teaching easier and more fun. Let it give you the jump start you need to be a better teacher every day—starting now!

1

Classroom
Teaching Tips

1.

Be flexible. "Schedule" a little spontaneity into your lesson plans to take advantage of the "teachable moment."

2.

Pace yourself. You have to stay ahead of the fastest student and remain right alongside the slowest pupil at the same time.

3.

Use peer tutors in your classroom. When kids teach other kids, everyone wins.

4.

Teach all students a simple six-step
problem-solving process:

- Identify the problem.
- Define limits.
- Clarify issues.
- Search for solutions.
- Take action.
- Evaluate results.

5.

Set routines. They work wonders. Kids
thrive on structure and work better
when they know what's coming.

6.

Get new students off to a positive start by providing a "New Kid Kit" containing a school map, daily schedule, class picture, class roster, and a free lunch coupon.

7.

In today's world of sound bites and short attention spans, old-fashioned proverbs are being rediscovered. Use them to teach important life-lessons. Better yet, have kids make up their own to share their understanding of the world.

8.

Fight boredom! After all, you're competing with MTV.

9.

Help your students get organized and stay organized. Organization is one of life's survival skills. Using a lesson reminder book is a good way to start.

10.

Break down gender stereotypes. Bring in women scientists and mathematicians as role models for young girls. Help your female students break the "glass ceilings" in schools.

11.

Vary activities often. You may like to listen to yourself lecture for an hour or more, but your students won't. They're used to commercials and station breaks.

12.

Build a winning classroom—one child at a time. You can teach an entire class only by focusing on individual learners.

13.

Teach goal setting as a survival skill. Children don't know that setting goals can change their lives unless we tell them.

14.

Make room for fun in your classroom. Learning is important, but it shouldn't be deadly serious all the time. If education isn't fun, kids aren't going to want any.

15.

Show students that computer spelling check programs only recognize if letters make a word. They can't tell if it's the right word. Only an educated person can do that.

16.

Try a little mood music in your classroom. It can help you create the proper atmosphere for any learning activity.

17.

Expect students to do "real" work. Pride comes from accomplishment, not charity.

18.

Do whatever it takes to connect kids with computers. Arrange for loaners or check out units if necessary. Every student—not just wealthy or middle-class students—needs access to technology.

19.

Encourage study groups in and out of
the classroom. When kids team up on
learning, ignorance doesn't have a
chance.

20.

Be a booster for journal writing. Keeping
a journal is a good way for students to
vent feelings, express creativity, and
practice writing skills at the same time.

21.

Allow pupils to dig deeply for
knowledge. Today's learners need depth
as well as breadth. Shallowness isn't a
world-class standard. Occasional in-
depth investigations will prepare
students to compete in the world arena.

22.

The first three rules of effective teaching are (1) Praise; (2) Praise; and (3) Praise! But praise students only for honest effort and authentic accomplishment. Phony praise can lead to false pride and failed dreams later on.

23.

Foster intergenerational learning experiences in your classroom. When all generations learn and play together, everyone grows.

24.

Don't let a single textbook define your curriculum. Teach students to use a variety of materials (resource-based instruction) in order to get a well-rounded and well-grounded learning experience. Learning shouldn't be one-dimensional.

25.

Use assessment to drive instruction in your classroom. Let test results help you help students better. That's what test scores are for, not for penalizing or embarrassing students.

26.

Teach to a variety of learning styles. Kids don't all learn in the same way. The more you mix and match teaching techniques, the more likely you are to help all learners succeed.

27.

Refuse to inflate grades. Young people need honest feedback, not exaggerations. Kids can take reality. They just can't take lies from adults they trust.

28.

Don't rely solely on tests to tell you what your pupils can do. Students are more than scores. Find a variety of ways (for example, writing samples, performance on tasks, or artwork) for students to demonstrate their knowledge. Artists use portfolios to represent the variety and range of their body of work. Why not compile student portfolios for the same purpose?

29.

Minimize "downtime" in the classroom. Strive to have worthwhile learning activities going on every minute. Students attend more regularly when they are afraid they will miss out on something important.

30.

Emphasize cooperative learning in your classroom. Today, kids need to learn that in school and in life many problems are best solved when people work together, rather than competing against each other.

31.

Urge students to trade books. It's a way to stretch budgets and multiply exposure at the same time. It works with baseball cards.

32.

Use an interdisciplinary approach whenever you can. That's the way the real world works. Life happens all at once, not in separate compartments.

33.

Teach students to use visualization (imaging) techniques. It's a form of mental rehearsal. What you can visualize, you may achieve.

34.

If a lesson isn't working, don't do more of it. Do something else—quickly. Bad lessons don't get better by themselves. Always have a backup plan in reserve.

35.

Learn to give instructions in sound bites. It's what today's kids are used to.

36.

Make all your lessons as
multicultural, inclusive, and
gender-fair as possible. Good
teaching leaves no one out.

37.

Despite today's media and political
infatuation with "sound bites," continue
teaching solid writing skills. Even the
Internet could benefit from clear,
effective writing.

38.

Allow adequate "wait time" for students
to respond to questions. Don't rush to
fill the void if no one volunteers an
answer immediately. A little silence puts
subtle pressure on students to come
forward with what they know.

39.

Saturate your classroom with volunteer readers. The more adults who read to children, the more likely children are to read as adults.

40.

Schedule the hardest lessons when students are freshest. That's why some schools are delaying their start time for senior high students to capitalize on periods of peak performance.

41.

Show students how to set up their own filing system at home. It's never too early for kids to start relying on "files, not piles."

42.

Let your students grade themselves occasionally. Have them fill out a report card on themselves and review it with you. Discuss areas where you disagree.

43.

No matter what reading program your school uses, insist on including some phonics. It's the only way to assure that students have lifelong decoding skills. A "whole language" approach can't do that.

44.

Periodically, ask your students, "How can we do better as a class?" Discuss their suggestions as a group.

45.

Teach students to respect and protect the planet and its resources. It will take only one generation of ecology-conscious citizens to make peace with the environment.

46.

Be a fanatic about books. Read them aloud. Read them silently. Display them. Talk about them. The more you are a cheerleader for books, the more likely your students are to catch "reading fever."

47.

Teach basic school survival skills such as memory aids, test-taking techniques, note-taking skills, and proofreading tips. These skills help set up students for success.

48.

Celebrate successes—even little ones! Encouragement is never wasted.

49.

Remember that more isn't always better. The teacher who talks the most or assigns the most doesn't always teach the most.

50.

Build students' vocabularies—no matter what subject you're teaching. Words are power. It's yours to give.

51.

Bring real authors into your classroom (if only by the Internet). Live interaction between students and published writers makes kids want to read and write more. Surprisingly, it has the same effect on the professionals as well.

52.

Be approachable. Being seated behind a desk is not a welcoming position. Get up, get out, and mingle with "your people." It works for politicians and it can work for you.

53.

Give students more practice in planning, thinking, and deciding and less practice in memorizing, copying, and repeating.

54.

Begin and end class on time—every time. Punctuality teaches a lesson. Besides, it's your job.

55.

Never teach a weak lesson twice. Fix it.

56.

Make a big deal over discouraging plagiarism. Copying from the Internet is easy, but it robs students of the joy of original work.

57.

Never use a worksheet when an open-ended question would work better.

58.

Always have good lesson plans for substitute teachers. The practice of throwing unsuspecting victims to the lions went out of fashion a long time ago.

59.

All good stories have a "hook" to capture the reader's interest from the very beginning. Good lessons are the same way.

60.

Don't always call on the kids who hold up their hands. It lets all the others off the hook too easily.

61.

Keep your method of determining grades simple. It shouldn't take a CPA to figure out your marking system.

62.

Give your kids a break once in a while—no weekend homework!

63.

Realize that students are always learning; even recess is part of their curriculum.

64.

Get *everyone's* attention before you start a lesson. It's worth the wait.

65.

Sometimes, books are the best teachers.
Here are two modern classics: *Old Turtle*
by Douglas Wood (Pfieffer-Hamilton
Pub.) teaches respect for diversity and
the environment; and *The Next Place* by
Warren Hanson (Waldman House Press)
offers comfort to those grieving the loss
of a loved one.

66.

Tell your classes about former students
who have gone on to lead successful
lives. Kids respond to examples and role
models. They need to know that
achieving success can still happen.

67.

Praise students in public. Criticize them in private. Never subject a child to public humiliation. That's the number one complaint of students everywhere.

68.

Don't be a slave to your syllabus. Reaching just one student is more important than finishing a dozen textbooks.

69.

Always have more to offer. When students have mastered the lesson at hand, there should be another place for them to go intellectually.

70.

Be willing to arrive early and stay late—
maybe even come in on Saturday once
in a while—to help students who really
want it and need it. If a pupil is ready to
learn, a teacher should be ready to teach.

71.

Know the difference between teaching
and sermonizing.

72.

Revisit your best lessons. Why did they
work? What can work again? There's no
rule against repeating success.

73.

Remember that short, direct instructions and explanations work best. There's a reason why teachers aren't paid by the word.

74.

Set up a "Fix-It Station" in your classroom where students can repair projects that get torn or broken or come unglued or get disassembled.

75.

Keep a supply of brainteasers and puzzles on hand for the kids who always finish before the rest of the class does. When students are ready for more, they should get it.

76.

Try scheduling the study period at the beginning of class, instead of at the end. The students will be fresher, and they may not waste so much time clock-watching.

77.

Teach students that sentences get cluttered too. Eliminating litter applies to language as well as to the environment.

78.

Keep green plants in the classroom. They add beauty (as well as oxygen) and make the learning space seem less institutional.

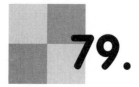

79.

When you have to give a failing grade, try to make it clear that the work is unsatisfactory, not the student.

80.

You can't prepare students for an essay-test world with a fill-in-the-blanks curriculum. Think about it!

81.

Handle each student paper only once. "Working smarter" will keep you from second-guessing yourself and save you time as well.

82.

Teach your students that one way to get the right answers is to ask the right questions. There's no such thing as a stupid question—as long as it reflects a sincere desire to learn.

83.

Incorporate some poetry into your daily lessons. Otherwise, some kids may never experience the power of a poem. That would be a shameful loss.

84.

Conduct a vision audit of your classroom. Check sight lines, glare, and blind spots. An obstructed view creates frustration and distraction.

85.

When the weather is too nice to stay inside, don't. A little fresh air and sunshine never hurt any lesson.

86.

Don't worry about defending or explaining what you do. Good teaching speaks for itself.

87.

Keep an instant camera in your classroom. There are always plenty of special moments to photograph and post, keep, or send home.

88.

The secret to good teaching is timing. You want to catch the student somewhere between "I can't believe I don't know this" and "It doesn't matter anymore."

89.

Give students continuous feedback. No poor grade should ever come as a surprise.

90.

Turn nonteaching chores into real-world learning experiences. Assign a student to take roll and learn how to compute percentage of attendance at the same time. Put students in charge of the class fund-raiser and teach them how to "keep the books." Not all lessons have to come from textbooks.

91.

Don't merely teach how to spell a word. Teach why it is spelled that way as well.

92.

For those students who are reluctant to give oral reports, try a historical "wax museum" project. Have each pupil select and research a historic figure, prepare a brief report, dress in costume, and recite whenever someone presses his or her "start button." It seems like a game, but it's really good practice in giving oral presentations. No one ever said teachers can't be sneaky.

93.

When planning your lessons, don't always save the best for last. You may run out of time.

94.

Expect excellence. Accept best effort.

95.

Don't just give students something to do. Give them something to think about.

96.

Don't rule out memorization. It's still a valuable teaching tool. What's worth remembering is worth memorizing.

97.

Don't waste too much time on spelling bees. Why give the most practice to those who need it least?

98.

Pay attention to climate control in the classroom. Temperature, humidity, and ventilation affect student performance. Part of good teaching is providing a "comfort zone" for learning.

99.

For a refreshing way to review for a quiz, have students take turns playing radio talk-show host and let the rest of the class "call in" their questions.

100.

Hands-on science instruction energizes learning, but there are safety risks. Be sure your classroom has a Science Safety Kit containing rubber gloves, kitty litter for absorbing spills, and eye rinse.

101.

Use lots of stickers and stamps on student papers. They are shorthand for "I like your work."

102.

Don't let the first class after lunch be a lesson in lethargy. Spark things up with some "deskersizes" before starting the afternoon's work.

103.

Support alternative education. There are always students who need something different. No one approach fits all—not even yours.

104.

Don't be distracted by decorative artwork on student papers. Look for substance behind the glitz. Sometimes the best work comes in modest packages. Remember the story of Lincoln writing the Gettysburg Address on the back of an envelope?

105.

Kids love to beat their own record. Timing performances and charting progress are mighty motivators. When students compete against themselves, they always come in first.

106.

Along with Band-Aids, keep some spot remover and a sewing kit handy. Kids can't concentrate when they're worried about a stain, a missing button, or a torn shirt. Sometimes, kids' clothes need first aid too.

107.

Interrupt what you're doing to point out
a rainbow. Kids need to learn what you
have to teach, but many need a few
rainbows in their lives just as much.

108.

Check the acoustics in your classroom.
Eliminate sound barriers and
unnecessary background noise. (Research
shows that one-third of today's students
often miss up to 30 percent of all verbal
communications in schools.) A sound
education depends on being able to hear
the teacher.

109.

Don't mistake teaching faster for teaching better. There's a natural pace to learning. Speeding up often confuses students.

110.

Hit television shows can be popular in the classroom as well. "Jeopardy," "Wheel of Fortune," and "Who Wants to Be a Millionaire?" work well with all ages as vehicles for review. Who says learning can't be fun?

111.

Don't always seat students alphabetically or line them up by height. Think of the kids who are consistently put at the back of the room or at the end of the line. Everyone deserves to be first sometime.

112.

Take fire drills seriously. They're more than bothersome interruptions. Think of all the passengers on the *Titanic* who wished they'd paid closer attention during the lifeboat drill.

113.

Don't expect quantum leaps in student performance. Success is usually incremental. Learning, like baseball, is a game of inches.

114.

Occasionally, take a page from real life by using evaluative indicators that students readily recognize, such as "two thumbs up," "three out of five stars," or "7 on a scale of 1 to 10." After all, the purpose of feedback is communication.

115.

Just as libraries have amnesty periods for overdue books, set aside a window of time when students can hand in late assignments without penalty. In learning, late is better than never.

116.

Welcome standardized tests and national assessments. They help us focus. In the words of Tom Peters, "What gets measured, gets done."

117.

Be open to visiting teachers from other species. Sometimes a fly on the wall or a colony of ants on the playground can teach lessons more important than the ones you had planned for the day.

118.

Have your students bury a time capsule containing popular school items of the day. It's a gift of history that today's students can give to tomorrow's learners.

119.

Problem-solving ability is mostly a matter of attitude. Teach students that problems are friends. Without them, there would be no challenge, no learning, and no triumph.

120.

Send a welcome-back postcard to each student the week before school starts. It's an easy way to get kids "hyped-up" about the new school year.

121.

Sometimes let your students write the test items. You'll probably end up with tougher questions and fewer complaints about them.

122.

Minimize transition time. Teach students to settle down quickly, to start work promptly, and to wrap up without dawdling. It's a way to lengthen the school day without changing the starting or ending time.

123.

Incorporate a "Mission Impossible" theme into your lessons. Place enrichment exercises on cassette tapes introduced by the familiar "Your mission, should you choose to accept it, is . . ." Good teachers aren't above using gimmicks.

124.

Videotape a series of supplemental lessons for use by substitute teachers. The tapes will help preserve your presence in the classroom and make things run more smoothly in your absence.

125.

Use cartoons to teach the proper use of quotation marks. Even young students can learn that the words inside a speech balloon in a cartoon or comic book should be inside quotation marks in written work.

126.

Take a tip from people who stock grocery shelves. Place the best references at eye level where kids will see them and pick them up first. Place less frequently used resources on higher or lower bookshelves.

127.

Is your list of basic school supplies up-to-date? Paper, pencils, paste, crayons, and scissors aren't enough anymore. Many schools now require computer and DVD disks as well.

128.

If you're having difficulty getting students to write, try holding a "Liar's Contest" instead of giving a "canned" creative writing assignment. You'll be surprised how quickly student interest perks up.

129.

Stress the importance of preparation. An unprepared student is just a failure waiting to happen.

130.

In many of their songs, the Beatles referred to actual places where they had once lived in Liverpool. Use examples from popular songs to show students the importance of writing about things they know firsthand. Who says that rock and roll can't be educational?

131.

Turn data-gathering into a scavenger hunt for information. The first student to find all the facts on the list wins. There's no reason that the "grunt work" of learning has to be boring.

132.

Whatever subject you teach,
include some career information.
You never know when
unsuspecting students will stumble
across their life's work.

2

Student Relations

133.

Don't be conned by kids. Never believe everything students tell you about what other teachers do or allow in their classrooms.

134.

Be silly with your students sometimes. They need to know you're human too.

135.

Treat all students alike—fairly. There are no favorites in a master teacher's classroom.

136.

Be a cheerleader for all your students. Cheer loudest for the children who have the fewest fans in their corner.

137.

Dare to touch kids. They need it more than ever before. Hugging a child who needs it isn't sexual harassment. It's caring. And that's what good teaching is all about. (Note: To avoid any possible misunderstandings, always follow your school's guidelines regarding touching students.)

138.

What are the three best ways to teach respect and tolerance? Example. Example. Example.

139.

Don't tell students they have failed without also telling them where they can go for help and how they can still reach their goals. Good teachers never leave students stuck at a dead end.

140.

Remember, your classroom may be the only happy home some kids ever have.

141.

Downplay appearance. Help female students, especially, celebrate their individual talents and interests and establish their identity based on qualities other than appearance, popularity, and sexuality.

142.

Keep your word. If students can't trust their teacher, whom can they trust?

143.

Use the power of self-disclosure. If you open up to students, they will open up to you.

144.

Don't feel that you have to be everybody's buddy. Your students already have friends. What they need is a teacher.

145.

Be sure your students know where you stand on important issues such as drugs, gangs, bigotry, and violence. Students look to you for guidance. Give them some.

146.

Let your faith in teaching and learning guide your actions. Show your students that you believe all kids can learn. There are no throwaway kids in a master teacher's classroom.

147.

Avoid labeling children. Kids tend to live down to the labels adults give them.

148.

Expect the best. You'll probably get it. Teacher expectations often become self-fulfilling prophecies. Children (and adults) tend to live up to the success others predict for them.

149.

Let your students know that you won't back off or go away. When they find out that you won't give up on them or yourself, they won't either.

150.

Anticipate that students will search out and try to exploit your weaknesses. It's what they do best. Don't worry. You can handle it. You're the grown-up in the crowd.

151.

The day a child learns to read ranks right up there with the day she took her first step or got her first tooth. Celebrate accordingly.

152.

Don't feel that you always must have the answer to every student's problem. There are times when the most you have to offer is a tissue. Sometimes that's enough.

153.

Allow your students to have a bad day now and then. Allow yourself to have one too.

154.

If you must choose between working with papers and working with kids, choose kids every time!

155.

Be consistent and avoid sending mixed messages. Students shouldn't have to guess which teacher is going to show up.

156.

Think like a child. Act like an adult.

157.

When you refer students for special help, be sure it's for their benefit, not just for your convenience.

158.

Support extracurricular activities.
They are the allies, not the
competitors, of the classroom.
Many students are drawn by the
activities and end up achieving in
academics as well.

159.

Don't just pick a "student of the week." Pick a group of pupils each week. That way, everybody can be included sometime during the year. It doesn't hurt anyone to be recognized. It does hurt to be left out.

160.

Don't patronize students. They may not know what to call it, but they'll know what you're doing and they'll hate it.

161.

Don't promise what you can't deliver. Raising false hopes isn't fair to students.

162.

Display a banner that says "Welcome" in all of the native languages represented in your classroom. All kids can learn, but first they must feel accepted.

163.

Never stifle or belittle a child's imagination. Good teachers are dream-makers, not dream-busters.

164.

Set your students up for success. (It may be a new experience for some of them.) Once students know what success feels like and what it takes to get it, they'll take it from there.

165.

Realize that critical-thinking skills aren't just for gifted students. All kids can learn how to think better.

166.

Never define any child by an IQ score. There are lots of different kinds of intelligence. They all count.

167.

Give students many choices. Making choices sharpens their teeth for biting off bigger decisions later.

168.

Remember that "tough love" applies to teaching too. Sometimes doing what seems unfair and unreasonable is really in your students' best interests. Do what's right—even if it hurts for a little while.

169.

Build on strengths. Continually dwelling on weaknesses is discouraging for you and for your students.

170.

Don't lend or give students money for lunch. If necessary, buy them lunch tickets. That way, you're sure how the money has been spent.

171.

Teach students to trust and value their own instincts. If they're uncomfortable doing something, they need to have the self-confidence to say no.

172.

Never tease students unless you know they enjoy it. What seems funny to an adult may be intimidating or embarrassing to a child.

173.

For a novel way to recognize outstanding students, try affixing their picture to a Wheaties box. That's where champions belong.

174.

Be honest with students. If you always
tell the truth, you don't have to try to
remember your lies.

175.

Don't expect students to look up to you
if you talk down to them.

176.

Never jump on a student's idea before it
has a chance to fly.

177.

Keep giving your students signs that show you care (for example, thumbs-up, a nod, a wink, a touch). You can't assume kids know how you feel. Caring about them and respecting them are the qualities students want most in a teacher.

178.

Be allergy-conscious. Some students have severe reactions to latex. Maintaining a healthy environment for all pupils may mean banning balloons from the classroom.

179.

The most precious gift you have to give is your time. Give some to each student every day.

180.

Enjoy your students. It's the only way to survive as a teacher. They will disappoint you sometimes. They may even break your heart at times. More often, they will surprise, amaze, and delight you. Those are the moments that make it all worthwhile.

181.

Tell students about your home life. Show family photos. Share the fun you have with your spouse and children. Some kids need to know that a happy family is a possibility.

182.

Eat lunch with your students now and then. You'll be surprised what you can learn from "dinner-table conversation" at school.

183.

Use more terms that unify (*we, us, together*) and fewer divisive words such as *me* and *mine*.

184.

If a student brings you a problem you can't handle, don't handle it. Refer it to the appropriate specialists. Know your limits.

185.

Be realistic. When early adolescents have to choose between hormones and homework, hormones win almost every time. Don't give up. Try to keep students focused. Make assignments lively and interesting. Most of all, remain patient. Kids can learn in spite of puberty.

186.

Be your best when your students are at their worst! Show sensitivity in times of special family situations or needs, such as a job loss, divorce, physical or sexual abuse, loss of a loved one (including pets), or drug problems in the home.

187.

Everyone needs leadership training and experience. Don't always pick the same kids to lead.

188.

Don't look down on kids with tattoos or pierced body parts. Fashion is neither good nor bad. Beauty and "cool" are in the eye of the beholder.

189.

Never walk away from a child who has no place to go.

190.

Accept that your students can have ideas that are as good as or better than yours. Do it their way sometimes.

191.

Get involved with students outside the classroom. Attend some of their activities. Have fun with them on their own turf. It does wonders for teacher-pupil relationships.

192.

Help your students see that it isn't just the disabled student who benefits from inclusion. All students benefit. Teachers do too.

193.

Respect what ethnic groups preferred to be called (for example, Latino, African-American, or Native American).

194.

Join your students in regular visits to a homebound classmate who has a long-term illness. It's scary to feel separated and isolated as a young person. Help the student to continue to feel a part of your class.

195.

Look at the pictures your students make. Drawings are a window to what kids are thinking and feeling.

196.

Let your students see you studying, reading, and working hard. Your everyday example is a powerful teaching tool.

197.

Ask students for their opinions—often!
Kids are often told; they are seldom
asked. They'll feel good that you cared
what they think, and you'll pick up some
valuable insights and ideas in the
process.

198.

Be an ombudsman for ornery kids.
Orneriness can simply be another form
of creativity. Think of how many
brilliant and successful adults were once
troublemakers in school.

199.

You don't have to love every student, but
they don't know that. Let it be your
secret.

200.

When tragedy strikes your school (for example, the death of a student or faculty member), don't act as if it's business as usual. It isn't. Allow pupils to talk about their feelings. Permit grieving. It's a natural reaction.

201.

Startle your students with your peripheral vision. (It can be improved through practice and exercise.) Classroom management is easier when students think you have "eyes in the back of your head."

202.

If you're afraid of bugs, don't show it.
Students love to torment teachers about
their fears.

203.

Watch the comparisons you make.
Military metaphors such as "take no
prisoners" or "troops in the trenches"
work well for competitive situations, but
not for a classroom built on respect,
cooperation, and goodwill.

204.

Don't always feel you have to make a
point or teach a lesson every minute of
the day. Sometimes a little friendly
conversation with a caring adult is what
some students need most.

205.

Take student talk about suicide seriously. If a threat is immediate, intervene calmly and call 911. If it is not immediate, have someone stay with the student and call the parents or the student's doctor (or follow the school policy, if there is one). If needed, the National Suicide Hotline number is 1-800-784-2433.

206.

It is not your job to make every child like you. It is your job to make all children like themselves a little better.

207.

Let students with attention deficit disorder (ADD) know that they aren't crazy or stupid. They just process information differently. Life with ADD is a little harder, but it is definitely more interesting.

208.

Don't spend too much time fault-finding. Blaming is looking backward. Solutions require moving forward.

209.

When you see students who are "natural teachers," encourage them. It's never too early to start recruiting tomorrow's miracle workers.

210.

Don't merely respond to what students ask. Answer the questions they may be afraid to ask because they don't want to be embarrassed or look dumb. Good teachers need a touch of ESP. It comes with experience.

211.

Never think of students as "the enemy." It's your job to fight *for* them, not with them.

212.

As a teacher, you have countless decisions to make every day, but only one standard to apply: what is best for kids.

213.

Don't just notice the kids who are in your face all the time. Pay attention to those children huddled on the sidelines as well.

214.

If you don't expect students to be
perfect, they will never disappoint you.

215.

Mix the cliques. Don't allow the same
self-selected cliques to work together all
the time. Rearrange groups so that all
pupils experience diversity.

216.

Teaching and learning are not always
reciprocal. You count on your students,
but sometimes they let you down. They
count on you, but you can never let
them down.

217.

Businesses use exit interviews. Why not schools? When students leave your class in midyear, ask them what worked, what didn't, and why.

218.

Watch for the child who's having a bad day. You can turn it around. Smile. Say or do something nice. You can be a day-brightener for any child.

219.

It's OK for kids to have a crush on their teacher. It's not OK for teachers to encourage it. Always make it clear that you're the teacher—nothing more, nothing less.

220.

Avoid comparing siblings. No child should have to start out being "second best" or found guilty by bloodline.

221.

Have a short memory for mistakes, failures, and behavior slips. Every child deserves a fresh start each morning.

222.

On a good day, students will surprise you. On a bad day, students will surprise you. Don't be surprised by surprises.

223.

No matter how long you teach, don't think you've seen it all. There isn't any "all." Students come in infinite variety.

224.

Never refuse to give individual help when asked by a student who really needs it. Find the time. Find the energy. Find a way. Anything less is unacceptable.

225.

Don't underestimate your students' maturity level. Let them make decisions commensurate with their comfort zone. Teachers are supposed to stretch students, not restrain them.

226.

If you have occasion to buy a present for a student, give a learning gift. Books and magazine subscriptions always make good gifts from teachers.

227.

If students hang around your classroom before and after school, they must want to talk. Make it easy. Break the ice. Reach out before they lose their nerve and you lose an opportunity to teach or help.

228.

Recognize and reward all students. All children deserve some time in the sun.

229.

Telling bad jokes is common to students of all ages. Laugh at their childish attempts at humor. After all, they laugh at yours.

230.

Make sure every child feels he or she "belongs" in your class. Exclusion and ostracism among students are common in schools. Often, kids who feel left out become depressed and desperate. It happened in Columbine. Don't let it happen in your school.

231.

Give students formal recognition (letter grades) at least once a week. Give informal recognition (a kind word or a pat on the back) every day!

232.

Relive the wonder of first-time experiences. What's "old hat" to you is brand new for students. If teachers become blasé, children are cheated out of sharing the thrill of discovery.

233.

On the last day of school, give each child an envelope to open in midsummer. Inside, write "I miss you but will see you soon." For some kids, reading your message may be the best thing that happens to them all summer long.

3

Student Discipline and Classroom Management

234.

Structure the classroom space so you can move around easily and get close to every student. (Try a U-shape arrangement.) Be everywhere in your classroom.

235.

Allow some constructive noise in the classroom. Noise can actually help settle down restless students. Dr. Harlen Hensen of the University of Minnesota explains, "Good noise means learning. Bad noise means the children are out of control. No noise means adults don't understand the nature of children."

236.

Reserve a "limbo seat" in the classroom
for any student who can't function or
focus in his or her regular seat for the
day.

237.

Establish a student grievance procedure
in your classroom and hold periodic
"sound off" sessions so students can vent
frustrations and identify problems.

238.

Don't be a historian. Avoid prejudging
students on the basis of past experience
or family history.

239.

Don't rush to medicate bad behavior.

240.

Put safety first. Make your classroom a safe haven for every child. Insist on zero tolerance for fighting, bullying, or harassment. If kids don't feel safe, they can't learn.

241.

Practice amnesty. The best teachers give lots of second chances and don't bear grudges.

242.

Teach conflict resolution skills—
active listening, positive body
language, brainstorming solutions,
and others—as an alternative to
violence. Kids need to learn how
to settle disputes peacefully both in
and out of the classroom.

243.

Always present classroom rules with conviction. Avoid any hint of questioning, hesitancy, timidity, uncertainty, pleading, or negotiating. If students think there's some wiggle room, they'll wiggle. Take your rules seriously and your students will too.

244.

Discipline tip: When problems occur, have the students involved call their parents in your presence to report the trouble, rather than calling yourself. You'll be surprised what a difference it makes when everybody hears the same story at the same time.

245.

Try not to "lose it" no matter how much you're tested. If students see they've angered you, they know they've beaten you at the discipline game.

246.

Keep reminding yourself that the most unpleasant student you have is probably the one who needs you most.

247.

Use a variety of positive reinforcers, such as free computer time, being first in line, or time to sit with a friend, to motivate students. "Whatever works" is always the best choice.

248.

Get by with as few rules as possible.
Make 'em simple and make 'em stick.

249.

Don't waste time walking on eggs or
soft-pedaling consequences. Say what has
to be said and move on.

250.

Avoid sarcasm It seldom helps and often
hurts—a lot!

251.

Never punish children because you don't
like their parents. Kids are not
responsible for how their parents behave.

252.

Document all your disciplinary actions.
Notes and records are important in
today's litigious society. A good paper
trail can lead you out of a lawsuit.

253.

Don't confuse zero tolerance with zero
common sense. A kindergartener with a
water gun is not the same threat as a
teenager with a loaded revolver.

254.

Do enforce zero tolerance for racial or
sexist slurs. Let your classroom be a
model for what life should be like
everywhere.

255.

Avoid practicing entrapment. Don't bait or tempt kids to cheat. Leaving the classroom while a test is in progress is not a good idea. Teaching isn't intended to be a sting operation.

256.

Never look the other way when you suspect physical or sexual abuse. A child's safety may be a matter of life and death.

257.

Don't punish students when you are angry or grade papers when you are overly tired. Your students deserve you at your best.

258.

Learn the signs of gang presence and report them when you spot them in your school or community. Gangs are only as strong as the community allows them to be.

259.

Deny denial. If you think intimidation, stalking, harassment, or extortion never occur in your school, you're not paying attention. Face up to real problems. Seek real solutions.

260.

Discipline with your eyes. Looks can't kill, but they can inflict pain.

261.

When you feel overwhelmed, take your teaching one day at a time. If you deal successfully with today, you will always be ready for tomorrow.

262.

Be aware of what's going on around you. Schools aren't always safe places to be—especially after school hours and after dark.

263.

Don't repeatedly nag or plead with students. If they don't respond after two requests, take appropriate action.

264.

Remember that due process is for everyone. All students have a right to advance notice, a full hearing, and access to appeal.

265.

Model precaution. It's an important survival skill. Always lock up valuables. Unattended classrooms are easy targets for amateur (and professional) thieves.

266.

Use individual contracts with difficult students and parents to spell out discipline expectations and consequences. People respect contracts. There is power in a document you have to sign.

267.

"Racial profiling" isn't just a police problem. It can occur in schools too. Don't let it happen in yours. You know better.

268.

Be careful what you write about students and keep in your files. Don't assume that your personal notes are private. The power of the subpoena is far-reaching today.

269.

Watch for signs of sexual harassment in the classroom. If in doubt, apply this three-step test: Would you want your child treating others this way? Would you want a member of your family treated this way? Would the behavior be offensive if it were viewed by people you respect and trust?

270.

If you suspect students are cheating on tests, simply reverse the order of the questions or use different forms for different individuals or groups. Don't tempt fate (or weak students).

271.

Whenever students line up, always stand at the back of the line. It's better to see what's going on ahead of you than to trust what's happening behind you.

272.

Don't be naive. Some kids today are ruthless and remorseless. They pose a real threat. Don't think you're invincible or assume that you can work wonders with everyone. Some students are more than you can handle. They need special help. Be alert. Know your limits. Don't do anything stupid that may put you or your pupils in danger.

273.

When a student presents a behavior problem, ask last year's teacher what worked. It saves a lot of trial and error. There's no copyright on successful classroom management techniques.

274.

Have a reason, not just an excuse, for
everything you do in the classroom.

275.

Report all suspicious-looking packages or
objects. "Good things" may come in
small packages, but so do bombs.

276.

You know you're a good teacher when
your students do what they're supposed
to do, even when you're not looking.

277.

Teach kids that reporting drugs or
weapons in school isn't snitching. It's
survival!

278.

When disciplining students, use suspension sparingly. For some kids, it's a reward.

279.

Start and end each day with some comfortable rituals. Kids need anchors to stay focused and to reduce internal stress.

280.

Never try to shout over a noisy classroom. Talk "under the noise" instead. Factory workers first learned this trick on the assembly line in World War II.

281.

Your responsibility doesn't end at your classroom door. If you spot trouble anywhere in the school, it's not someone else's problem. It's yours.

282.

Don't get into a shouting match with students. You can't win, and you may lose your dignity and respect in the process.

283.

Dare to be a teacher who tests everything. If it's important, it's worth measuring. If it's unimportant, you shouldn't be teaching it anyway.

284.

Don't give students your home E-mail address unless you're open to anonymous insults, obscenities, and other assorted "cyber garbage."

285.

Learn the difference between a fair warning and an idle threat.

286.

Don't penalize children for being children. Wiggling and asking "why" constantly are natural behaviors, not misbehaviors.

287.

Balance praise and criticism.
Research shows that many teachers
spend much more time fault-
finding than in affirming their
students.

4

Working with Parents, Colleagues, and the Community

288.

Don't be too proud to scrounge for free stuff. You can't have too many resources for learning, and your classroom budget will never be big enough.

289.

Match up every student with a caring adult in the school or the community. Enlist custodians, secretaries, aides, and other staff and community members if necessary. It's important that all children have some grown-up who shows interest, follows their progress, pays attention, and is available to answer questions and discuss concerns.

290.

Help other teachers (particularly
beginners). It's not like you're movie stars
competing for the same roles. There are
plenty of kids and problems to go
around for everyone.

291.

Always use plain talk with parents. They
need answers, help, and direction, not
mumbo jumbo. Using big words and
jargon doesn't make you a better teacher.
Communicating clearly does.

292.

Don't forget about grandparents. Include and involve them in intergenerational school activities whenever possible. Grandparents make great aides, mentors, readers, storytellers, and listeners. They also bring a special patience, love, and wisdom into the classroom. What child couldn't use an extra grandma or grandpa?

293.

Make home visits. Good teachers don't hide in the school. If your students live in a rough neighborhood, take along a friend or ask a counselor or social worker to join you. If you can't visit every family, at least visit the homes of all newcomers and those students who are seriously falling behind.

294.

Start a "Catch-22" program in your classroom. Urge parents to "catch" at least twenty-two minutes of quality, one-on-one time with their child each day—reading, talking, or playing together. (Twenty-two minutes daily isn't much, but it's much more than the national average of thirty minutes a week.)

295.

Don't teach in a vacuum. Good teachers learn from each other. Network. Team teach. Find a way to connect with peers. Even competent professionals need a support group.

296.

Welcome other adults into your classroom for four good reasons: It's the best possible public relations policy. All students love an audience. Guests make the classroom seem more like part of the real world. You have nothing to hide.

297.

Don't be too hard on parents. They send you their very best, and most work hard at raising their kids. And they don't get summers off.

298.

Take time to serve as a broker of social services. See to it that your students' families get whatever kind of help they need. It's not in the job description, but it's part of the teaching life.

299.

Use native speakers and interpreters to inform and involve non-English-speaking parents.

300.

Go global. Network worldwide. There's no reason for any teacher to feel isolated anymore. Use E-mail and the Internet to exchange ideas with other teachers around the globe.

 # 301.

Urge that free transportation and child care be provided for all school functions involving parents. Serving a light meal is a good idea too. Make it easy for families to participate. Removing obstacles for parents is the school's part of the bargain.

302.

Be discreet. No one knows more family secrets than a teacher. Good teachers keep them.

303.

Involve all students in community-service learning projects. Marian Wright Edelman said it best: "Service is the rent we pay for living."

304.

Seek out a local business to adopt your classroom. The association will be good for your students and for the business as well.

305.

A whole generation of parents has grown up never hearing anything good about the public schools. It's your job to change all that.

306.

Encourage parents and students to sign a covenant to support learning and to work for better schools. People try harder when they're "under contract."

307.

Respect what parents know about their own children. Teachers don't always know best.

308.

Keep an up-to-date list of competent tutors to give to students or parents who need them. You can't help everyone all by yourself.

309.

Distribute a simple weekly or monthly parent newsletter. Parents can't help you or their child if they don't know what's going on at school.

310.

Establish clear-cut homework, make-up, and extra-credit policies, and see that all parents and students know what they are. It's unfair for anyone to be surprised by what counts and what doesn't.

311.

Coordinate your testing schedule with that of other teachers. There's no reason for students to have tests coming at them from all directions at once.

312.

Make friends with the school secretary and the building custodians. They can be your most important allies.

313.

Get your paperwork done on schedule. It doesn't take any more time to be on time, and it builds goodwill with people who count.

314.

Don't bad-mouth other teachers or the
school administration in public. You're
supposed to be on the same team.

315.

Don't take on other teachers' problems.
You'll have enough of your own.

316.

Be shameless. Copy what the best
teachers do, and don't feel guilty
about it.

317.

Tell parents what you would want to
know if their child were yours.

318.

Be sensitive about how much homework you assign. Remember that your students and their families have a life beyond schoolwork. Church, sports, scouts, fun, and family are important too.

319.

Take your share of "bad kids" and "dirty duty" (such as lunchroom supervision or bus loading). They are part of being a real pro.

320.

Don't expect your principal or your union to bail you out when you do something illegal, unethical, unprofessional, or harmful to kids. If you cross that line, you're on your own.

321.

Dare to conduct parent satisfaction surveys. If you aren't open to constructive criticism, how can you expect your students to be?

322.

Remind your colleagues that schools shouldn't be run for the convenience of adults.

323.

Practice good voice-mail etiquette.
Check messages frequently and respond
promptly. Good manners work just as
well when recorded as they do in person.

324.

Include noncustodial parents in school
mailings and classroom communications.
The child is theirs too.

325.

Develop special Parent Kits to help
families support their child's learning.
Include homework hints, summer
activity ideas, and tips on good books
for kids.

326.

Urge your principal to have all parent letters translated into the appropriate language for immigrant families in your school. Strangers in a strange land need all the help they can get. It might as well start with the school.

327.

Teach your students to treat substitute teachers as guests in the classroom. You want them to feel welcome so they'll accept your invitation to return when you need them. Assign one student to introduce the "guest" to the class in your absence and to review your daily routine for the sub.

328.

Have your students conduct their own parent-teacher conferences sometimes. It will "wow" the parents and make the kids more accountable.

329.

Don't assume that one kind of family is better than another. Some extended, mended, or blended families are stronger than many traditional ones.

330.

Make a big fuss over volunteers, aides, and substitutes. You couldn't do business without them.

331.

If parents don't want you to call them with problems, do it anyway. Don't let parents off the hook. They have to be involved and accountable too.

332.

Don't be too proud to bus tables or pick up litter. In a good school, everyone pitches in.

333.

Try holding a difficult parent conference in a neutral setting. How about meeting for coffee at a nearby fast-food restaurant?

334.

Don't be afraid to show off what your students have learned. The media never hesitate to exploit school failures. Schools should publicize their successes.

335.

Encourage parents to adopt a bus stop. Things go better when adults monitor the loading and unloading of school buses. A good day at school begins and ends with a safe bus stop.

336.

Have your students call parents, senior citizens, and other special "guests" with invitations to classroom events. Who can turn down a child's invitation?

337.

Respect parents' pocketbooks. Limit requests for money. It's unfair to assume that all families can afford expensive field trips or special school supply items. Be sure that no children in your classroom are ever embarrassed because their families are on a strict budget.

338.

Hold coffee parties or brown-bag lunch
sessions with parents. Informal contacts
help build bridges between the home
and the school.

339.

Conduct your class in a local mall once a
year. It's a great way for shoppers and
community members to see the school
in action.

340.

Never cover for an incompetent
colleague. Supporting a coworker is
one thing; enabling an unfit teacher to
damage children is another. You have
an obligation to all students, not just
your own.

341.

Lobby for a longer school year, but don't advocate taking summer completely away from children. Summertime is a special kind of education all by itself.

342.

With all the electronic wizardry at your command, don't forget one of the most versatile technologies of all—the telephone. Every classroom should have one. Use it often for up-close and personal contact with learning resources throughout the community and the world.

343.

Make a log of classroom disruptions (public address announcements, pull-out programs, etc.) for a one-month period. Use the results to lobby your principal for more uninterrupted instructional time. Students don't learn best in fits and starts.

344.

Don't blame last year's teacher for this year's problems. There's no reward for finger-pointing. Work with what you have and do your best. Good teachers don't need excuses.

345.

Listen to your own voice-mail greeting.
Is it upbeat and welcoming? Or flat and
impersonal? Make your first impression
(even if it's only an electronic one) a
good one.

346.

Pay attention to strangers in school.
Introduce yourself, ask if you can help,
direct them to the office, watch what
they do and where they go, and notice
details about their appearance. In violent
times, students in school can become
prey for predators. It's your job to
protect all the children.

347.

Urge parents to stay involved in their child's life, even through high school. It's a myth that adolescents are supposed to separate from their families and that parents are supposed to let them go. Teenagers and their parents need each other as much as ever—maybe more.

348.

Help parents and community members understand that just adding more tests is not educational reform.

349.

Don't treat parents like students. They are partners, not pupils.

350.

Listen to older teachers. They have wisdom and experience. Listen to younger teachers. They have exuberance and boldness. Listen most to yourself. You alone know what you want to do and what you can do.

351.

Recruit retired teachers to help children in your classroom. It will keep the retirees in touch. More important, it will make your students the beneficiaries of several lifetimes of successful teaching. What a gift!

352.

Some night, instead of giving homework, assign your students to spend the time with their parents. What family couldn't use the unexpected gift of an evening together?

353.

Ask your school to provide personalized business cards. They work for other professionals—why not teachers?

354.

Your school is only as strong as its weakest teacher. Do all you can to help that teacher get better. It's called being a professional.

355.

When attending professional conferences, set aside plenty of time for networking and informal contact with colleagues. These are often the best sources of new ideas, inspiration, healing, and growth.

356.

Don't be jealous of colleagues. Celebrate their successes and find out how they did it.

357.

If you join a team-teaching project, be sure it's for the right reasons. The goal should be to help kids learn better, not just to make your job easier.

358.

Urge the mayor of your town to convene a Youth Summit where students discuss issues that concern them most, while the adults listen without interrupting. When a community listens to its children, good things happen.

359.

Have your students send "Good Neighbor Awards" or thank-you notes to area residents. People who live around schools put up with extraordinary distractions. Let the neighbors know they are appreciated.

360.

Encourage parents to have a secret code word that must be given by any other adult who picks up their child from school. Precaution is part of doing business as a family today.

361.

Don't sign up for committees unless you plan to actively participate. It's unfair to other members. More important, you won't get anything out of it unless you put something into it. Dead wood doesn't grow.

362.

Don't leave everything for the custodian to do. Sometimes you and your class should clean up your own mess. It can be an important part of the lesson.

363.

Don't blame your problems on the state legislature. Nothing the government does (or doesn't do) will make you a better teacher.

364.

If you don't want parents telling you how to teach, don't tell them how to raise their children.

365.

Make friends with a pediatrician. You never know when you might need expert advice on a student's health-related learning problem.

366.

Ask school officials to conduct periodic tests to determine any dangerous levels of radon or carbon monoxide in the classroom. While you have their attention and cooperation, you might also ask them to check for asbestos and lead-based paints. Not all threats to students can be seen or smelled.

367.

Don't be duped into dispensing medications to students (not even an aspirin). Leave pharmacy functions to the school nurse. There are reasons why nurses follow strict guidelines. One of them is called "avoiding a lawsuit."

368.

Use a wristwatch alarm to keep parent conferences on schedule (for every sixty seconds one parent runs over, another is robbed of a minute of entitled teacher time).

369.

Support school uniforms. "Clothes wars" put pressures on kids and families, distract from learning, and generate snobbery in the classroom. Calvin Klein never helped anyone learn any better.

370.

Always have a wish list ready for parents, local businesses, the PTA, or anyone else who asks, "What do you need?" Good things come to those who are ready to receive them.

371.

Send something home to parents each week, but don't bury them in a paper blizzard every day.

372.

Know your community. It makes a
difference in what you teach and
how you teach it.

5

Personal Development and Motivation

373.

Organize your day—every day! Teaching shouldn't be a hit-or-miss affair.

374.

Be yourself. Kids can spot phonies. Being a good teacher isn't an act.

375.

Look your best. You'll feel better and teach better. Business people "dress for success." Why not teachers? (You'll be amazed how many of your students notice your earrings or necktie every day.)

376.

Have at least one silly rule for students
to test and protest. It makes it easier
for them to accept the rest of the limits
you set.

377.

Don't settle for sloppy or second best.
Excellence is always in fashion. The
"dumbing down" of America will
happen only if we let it. Don't let it.

378.

Put off procrastinating. You can't teach
students anything tomorrow. You can
only teach them today.

379.

Listen to yourself. Are you nagging?
Whining? Preaching? If you don't like
what you hear, do something about it.

380.

Don't act as though you're always in a
hurry. All children deserve someone who
has time for them.

381.

Associate with winners. Hang out with
the best teachers in your building.
Greatness rubs off. So does mediocrity.
Avoid the whiners and complainers.
You've got more important things to do.

382.

Be physically rested and ready for each
day. Students always have lots of energy.
You should too.

383.

Keep up with the latest technologies.
Learn from the kids if you have to.
If you're not up-to-date, you quickly
become irrelevant in today's classroom.

384.

Practice pacing and prioritizing. Save
time in your workday for advising,
planning, and professional growth.
Teaching is many things. Not all of
them occur in front of a classroom
full of kids.

385.

Don't take yourself too seriously. You're not the most important person in the classroom.

386.

Do whatever it takes to stay fresh throughout the entire school day (for example, don't skip breaks; practice stretching exercises; take mini mental vacations). The last lesson of the day deserves the same energy and enthusiasm as the first.

387.

Pay attention to complaints. They are another way to help you grow. Critics can be teachers too.

388.

Admit it when you don't know
something, and never hesitate to
ask for help when you need it. It's
OK for teachers to have warts.
Students are more comfortable
learning from real-life human
beings than from icons.

389.

Be aware of your body language. Sometimes your posture, gestures, or facial expressions speak louder than your words.

390.

Believe in miracles. They happen in your classroom every day!

391.

Get a life of your own outside of teaching. Both you and your students deserve it.

392.

Stay home when you're ill. That's what sick leave is for. Would you want a sick person teaching your child?

393.

Learn something new every day. Good teachers are good students first.

394.

Show that you like your job and your students. Your attitude provides the energy that drives the classroom.

395.

Talk less. Listen more. A big part of teaching is learning from your students.

396.

When your plate is full, don't take seconds. Learn to say no. It's a survival skill for busy teachers.

397.

Trust your instincts. If a course of action doesn't feel right, back off for a while.

398.

Save some time for reflection each day. Examine what you're doing and why. Have a plan. You want your teaching to be more than a series of knee-jerk reactions.

399.

Accept failure—your students' and your own. Learn from it and move on. As Zig Ziglar says, "Failure is an event, not a person."

400.

Remember why you became a teacher. It renews your commitment. The old reasons (love of kids, interest in helping others, and a desire to make a difference) still make sense.

401.

Work hard to make your teaching look easy.

402.

Don't expect to be appreciated right away. It often takes ten years after graduation for most people to realize how good their teachers really were.

403.

There is one important lesson they don't teach you in undergraduate school. Teaching is fun!

404.

Be a model of civility. Kids don't see enough of it in our society.

405.

Most kids start out loving school. Many end up disliking it. What do teachers do to take the joy out of learning in the interim? Think about it.

406.

Rehearse your lessons. It's not just students who need practice.

407.

Remember what it was like to be a student. This perspective will change the way you teach.

408.

Don't waste time telling people how good a teacher you are. Let results do your bragging for you.

409.

If your students are confused, ask yourself, "Who is confusing them?"

410.

Don't take work home every night. Your students shouldn't have homework seven nights a week and neither should you.

411.

Don't act childish when things don't go right. There's supposed to be an adult in every classroom. It's you!

412.

Recall all the dumb things your teachers did when you were in school—and don't do them.

413.

Ask yourself, "If school isn't fun, whose fault is it?"

414.

All teachers make mistakes. Good teachers admit it. Be one of the good ones.

415.

Remember that you don't have to be smarter than your students. You don't even have to be bigger than your students. But you should be more mature than your students.

416.

Look in the mirror and like what you
see. You have to feel good about yourself
before you can build your students'
self-esteem.

417.

Take care of your own children first, so
you can concentrate on taking good care
of other people's kids.

418.

Realize that master teaching is always a
work in progress. Times change.
Students change. Teachers must change
too. ("You can never step into the same
river twice." —Anon.) If you teach
tomorrow like you teach today, you
should have quit teaching yesterday.

419.

Dare to be different. Every teacher should have a unique "batting stance" in the classroom.

420.

Remember that the first step to successful teaching is to show up! Take your own attendance as seriously as you do your students'.

421.

Adopt this teacher's creed: "Don't blame. Don't shame. Know them by name. And let everyone play the game."

422.

Voluntarily change assignments
periodically. Try a new subject,
grade level, or school. People, like
plants, grow better if they are
repotted from time to time.

423.

Always respond to setbacks with renewed effort. Pouting, whining, or giving up are not effective teaching techniques.

424.

Stress lifelong learning. Not everyone goes to college, but life doesn't run out of lessons for any of us.

425.

Face your own prejudices. Be aware of how you treat people who are different from you.

426.

Remember that just because kids today
are seeing more, hearing more, doing
more, questioning more, and ignoring us
more doesn't mean they need us less.

427.

Don't rely on others for approval or
validation. You know when you've done
the right thing, and your students know
when you've helped them. That should
be enough.

428.

Remember that anything that makes you
a better person makes you a better
teacher too.

429.

Make good manners the way you do business in your classroom. It doesn't take any more time to be polite, and it makes working together a lot more pleasant.

430.

Think about the teachers who inspired you most. You can't be them, but you can find ways to be more like them.

431.

Be one of the best teachers who is still teaching his or her best on the last day of school.

432.

Work on your weaknesses. Keep trying to do better and to be better. Don't let a mediocre career just happen.

433.

Pay attention to your posture. Good posture keeps you fresh, boosts your confidence, and makes you look more like the teacher.

434.

If you take credit for your students' successes, be willing to accept some blame when they fall short.

435.

Don't be defined by your college major or limited by what it says on your teaching license. A good English teacher can teach a lot about health, and a good health teacher can teach a lot about English.

436.

Watch students entering and leaving your classroom. Their faces will tell you a lot about your teaching.

437.

Never give up hope. No good teacher can be a pessimist.

438.

Show pride in your school. Wear the school colors. Know the school song. Pride is infectious. Unlike most infections, however, pride makes individuals and organizations perform better.

439.

It's OK for teachers to get dirty in the line of duty. Don't worry about your appearance if you get mussed up or messed up helping children. God will forgive you—and so will the children.

440.

Be a squeaky wheel. Your students deserve as much grease as anyone.

441.

Pay attention to your penmanship. It matters. If scribbling is the best you can do, why should your students try to do any better?

442.

Refuse to become cynical. If you feel cynicism coming on, visit a nursery for newborns. Attend a confirmation class or a bar mitzvah. Go to a high school graduation. Kids and magic still go together. Teachers are part of that magic. Who can be cynical?

443.

Recognize the power of handwritten notes. Computer printouts, faxes, and voice-mail messages are fine, but personal notes, handwritten by the sender, carry more clout. Use them often.

444.

Stand up for what's right. Remember the teacher from Piper, Kansas, who resigned because the school board wouldn't back her in failing students who plagiarized their term projects. That's teaching by example.

445.

If your teaching doesn't leave time for your own learning, try enrolling in the "Automobile University." There are many educational tapes that can improve your knowledge and skill while you drive.

446.

Remember that each class of students is like a farmer's annual crop. Some are better than others, but they all take loving care in order to get the highest yield.

447.

Don't be too upset by what students say about you. Be more upset if they never talk about you at all. That means you're not having an impact on their lives.

448.

Be persistent. The secret of successful teachers is that they may fail frequently, but they never quit.

449.

Never put union matters, school politics, or career advancement before the interests of students. Children come first—period!

450.

Remember that you don't have to try
to be younger than you are in order to
teach young children. They will accept
you at any age if you will only act
your age.

451.

Think about the things that irritate and
frustrate you in the advanced college
courses you take. Avoid making the same
mistakes with your students. After all,
you should learn something in graduate
school.

452.

Remember the good times in the bad
times. It helps you know that things can
get better.

453.

Reread your childhood diary. It will remind you that relationships are sometimes more important than academics. That's why students aren't always as excited as you are about conjugating a verb or solving a math equation.

454.

Spend time with people who aren't teachers. If teachers talk only to other teachers, they begin to think that school and schooling are all that matter. They aren't. Kids know that. You should too.

455.

Take care of your feet. One secret of successful teaching is wearing comfortable shoes!

456.

Keep a little candy on hand. It can be a lifesaver for a diabetic child, a special treat for a student who deserves a reward, or a source of quick energy for a fading teacher.

457.

You don't have to be the best teacher in the school to be a success, but you have to be the best teacher you can be to avoid being a failure.

458.

Did you ever wonder how all the outspoken critics of education got so smart if schools are so bad? School-bashing isn't new. Don't take it personally. You know better than anyone else how good or how bad your school is.

459.

Just because you're having a bad day doesn't mean that your students must have one as well. Get a grip! Make something good happen for every child every day—even on your bad days.

460.

When you're low, remember that in most households, you are the most important person in the world outside the family circle. In emergencies, a doctor or plumber may temporarily be more important, but usually, the teacher is the most significant person beyond the immediate family. Who says teaching isn't a prestigious profession?

461.

Don't wear too much perfume or cologne. Some students are allergic. Besides, you may attract bees in season.

462.

Even if your school isn't ranked at the top, your classroom can be tops. Don't catch mediocrity from those around you.

463.

The good thing about teaching is that students are always watching you. The bad thing about teaching is that students are always watching you. If you don't like scrutiny, get out of teaching.

464.

If you think you can handle the truth, read Tracy Kidder's *Among School Children* or Elinor Burkett's *Another Planet*. They will force you to understand what it's like on the other side of the desk.

465.

"Use the past as a guide, not a leaning post." (Gordon Rausch, retired teacher)

466.

Teaching can be easy. Good teaching never is. Work hard at what you do. Earn the title of "Teacher."

467.

When you fall behind and the work is piling up, *refuse to panic*. Just do the next thing. And the next. Keep it up. Things will get better.

468.

Avoid the one cardinal sin all teachers fear committing—falling asleep in your own classroom.

469.

Keep fit. Your kids need you in top
shape. As the prolific source of wisdom,
"Anonymous," once asked, "If you ruin
your body, where will you live?"

470.

Remember that good teachers always
plan to be spontaneous and are a lot
better organized than they appear to be.

471.

"Near the end of the year, a teacher can't
help facing the fact that there's a lot she
hoped to do and hasn't done and now
probably never will. It's like growing old,
but for teachers old age arrives every
year." (Tracy Kidder, *Among School
Children*)

472.

To teach, stay teachable!

473.

Quit complaining about paperwork. Wherever there are teachers and students, there will always be papers to grade and reports to be made. Live with it.

474.

Don't be afraid of accountability. It's just a matter of promising only what you can deliver and delivering whatever you promise. You can do that.

475.

Just because you're not sure what you're doing doesn't mean that your kids have to know it. Sometimes bluffing is an essential survival skill for teachers.

476.

Guilt is destructive. Don't use it on students. Don't use it on parents. And don't use it on yourself.

477.

Don't become so specialized and compartmentalized that you can't help students with the basics in other subjects. When one teacher claims complete ignorance of another teacher's subject, students wonder why they should learn it.

478.

If teaching is just a job to you, you're merely a technician, not a real teacher. The difference is passion!

479.

Learn about the history of your school. This knowledge will help you convey a sense of pride and tradition to your students.

480.

Every teacher should coach or advise an after-school activity. Seeing each other in different roles and settings helps you and your students accept each other as human beings.

481.

Good schools don't happen by accident. Teachers make them that way. Are you doing your share to make the whole school better?

482.

Don't be afraid of competition, such as school choice, charter schools, or parent vouchers to attend private schools. Good teachers will always attract good students.

483.

You may be teaching English or math or music, but you are also showing kids what being an adult is like. How you act is as important as how you teach.

484.

Curriculum, materials, methods, and relationships determine the conditions of learning. Of these four, relationships are the most important.

485.

Don't ask if you can afford to get more training. You can't afford not to. A good teacher never knows enough.

486.

Find a spot in the school where you can enjoy absolute solitude for at least five minutes a day. Quietude is an elixir. A daily dose will help you feel better and teach better.

487.

Learn to write grant proposals. If you've got the ideas, someone else may have the money. Teachers get grants all the time. Why not you?

488.

If you don't get the transfer or special assignment you wanted, just make up your mind that it probably wasn't as good as it sounded anyway. Sour grapes are better than no grapes at all.

489.

Get a flu shot. Even the doctors on "ER" aren't exposed to as many germs as teachers are every day.

490.

Don't go back to graduate school every summer just to make more money. Go back to get better at what you do.

491.

Agree with your peers to pay a fine every time one of you uses the word "just" in conjunction with the statement "I am a teacher." If you don't respect your profession, who will?

492.

Pay attention to attendance. Yours. There will be days when you don't feel like teaching. Do it anyway. And do your best. Expect students to do the same.

493.

It's important to know the subjects you teach. But it's even more important to know your students and yourself.

494.

When someone compliments your teaching, reflect credit back on the kids and their parents. It's another touch of class that sets apart the truly great teacher.

495.

Never doubt that what you do is important. Firefighters and police officers save lives. But teachers save civilization. Teachers are heroes too.

496.

Sometime when you're working late and the building is quiet, listen to the voices of the ghosts of teachers past. They'll all tell you, "It's worth it!"

497.

What have you done for me lately?
When school starts, it doesn't matter
what success you had last year. You
haven't done anything for this year's
class yet. Teachers, like students, have
to prove themselves all over again every
year.

498.

Have some fun at work. Enjoy the silly
things kids do. Better yet, enjoy the silly
things the adults in the school do. No
one is exempt from a little foolishness
now and then.

499.

Don't rush out the door too soon on the last day of school. Pause to think about the year. What worked? What didn't? What will you do differently? A little quiet reflection will bring closure to the term, free you up for the summer, and set you up for a running start in the fall.

500.

Know when to quit. If you start to lose your caring or enthusiasm, it's time to graduate from teaching. No child deserves a burned-out teacher.

501.

Thank God you're a teacher. It
doesn't get any better than that.

About the Author

Dr. Robert D. Ramsey is a lifelong educator and freelance writer from Minneapolis. His professional career has included frontline experience in three award-winning school districts in two different states as a teacher, counselor, curriculum coordinator, personnel director, associate superintendent, acting superintendent, and adjunct professor.

Dr. Ramsey's previous publications include *501 Ways to Boost Your Child's Self-Esteem* and *501 Ways to Boost Your Child's Success in School*.

Through his popular writings, Dr. Ramsey has helped countless teachers and parents to understand, instruct, and inspire today's children and youth. *501 Tips for Teachers* is yet another tool that teachers can use to be their best and do their best for all students—every day!